DRAW WITH M

How to Use This Book:

Each page comes with a prompt for both mom and child to work. On some pages, you can work side by side at the same time, while on others it'll be encouraged that the child will draw first and then mom will add to their drawing. Each left page will have the child's prompt and each right page will have mom's. Please keep in mind that it <u>does not</u> mean that the left or right page is designated for one person or the other. In fact, we encourage both of you to draw on both pages (think of every two pages as one big page). On the bottom right corner of every right page, there will be a few conversation questions so you can chat while you draw!

LASTLY! At the very end of your book, you will each get a certificate! Yay!

A Few Tips for Moms

- Bring out your inner child! Show them how creative and imaginative you can get (we've included some ideas here and there in parenthesis next to your prompts, should you need some inspo:)!
- Don't be afraid to make things silly. Who knows maybe dinos had mustaches back in the day?
- If your child wants to do your part instead of theirs, you can always trade :).
- If there is still a lot of blank space on either page you can always add more detail or draw something else.
- Feel free to think outside of the box. If the prompt says to draw something specific but you and your little one decided on something else, that's okay! It's your book!

Your kind words and reviews are always appreciated ♡
Thanks for your support!

This Book Belongs to:

_____ **and** _____

Child: What's your favorite color in the rainbow? Draw the biggest rainbow ever!

Mom: Draw the sky around the rainbow. Then add more detail (like a pot of gold, unicorns, clouds made of cotton candy, etc.).

What do you like most about rainbows? Do you think there really are leprechauns at the end of the rainbow?

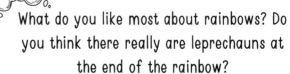

Child: Let's imagine it's a beautiful day at the farm! Draw a few animals you might see!

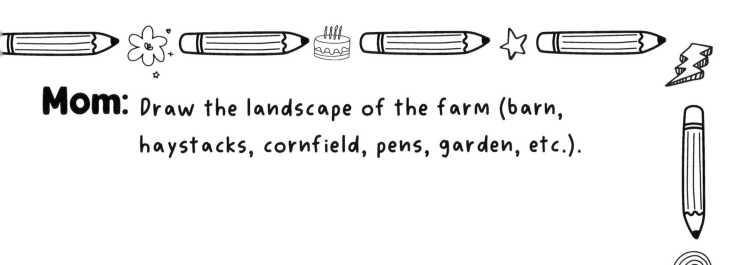

Mom: Draw the landscape of the farm (barn, haystacks, cornfield, pens, garden, etc.).

Do you like to visit farms? What's your favorite farm animal?

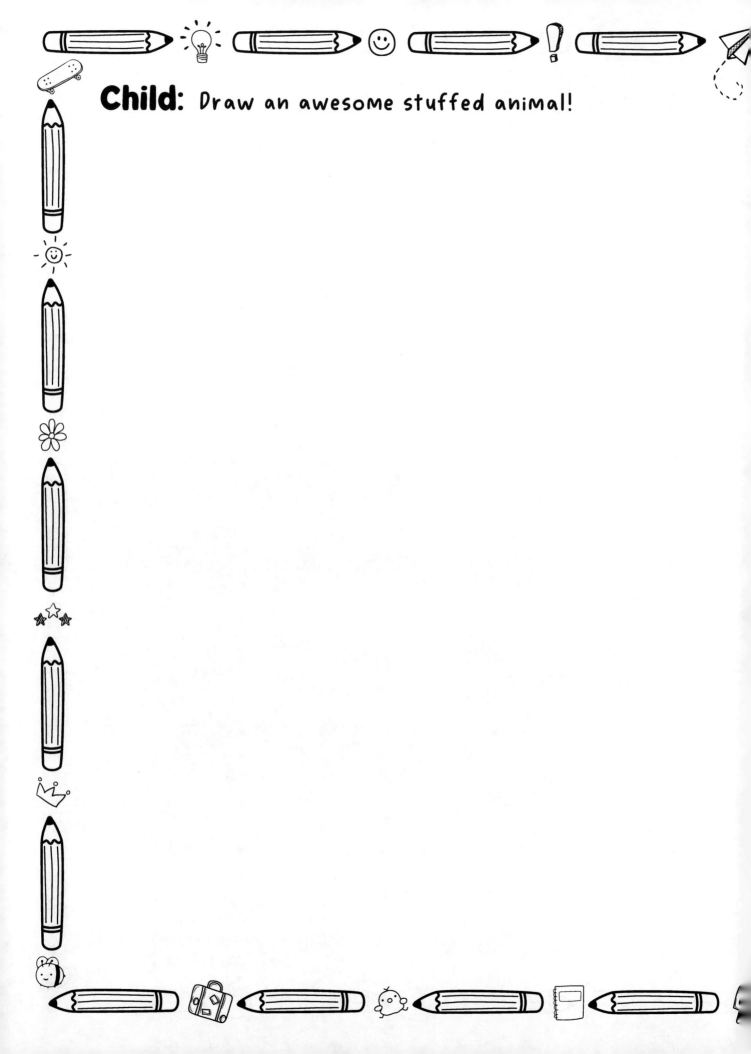

Child: Draw an awesome stuffed animal!

Mom: Add some unique features to your new furry friend to give them some character (like a bow tie, mustache, hair ribbon, etc.). Then draw a tea party set up for your stuffed animal.

(stuffed animal's name)

Do you have a favorite stuffed animal (mom did you have a favorite stuffed animal)? What is/was their name? What do/did you like most about your stuffed animal?

Child: Draw the biggest slide you can!

Woahhhhh that is huge!!!

Mom: Draw a few unique characteristics to the slide (like a water slide, slides into a ball pit, the slide transports you to another land, etc.).

Would you rather go on the super fast slide or a water slide? Do you like open slides or tunnel slides more?

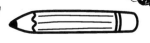

Child: Let's pretend to make a smoothie! Draw the ingredients you want to put in the smoothie.

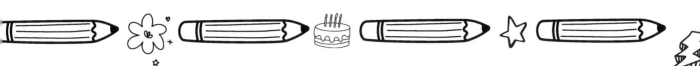

Mom: Add more detail to their smoothie drawing (like adding a veggie, drawing the blender, cups, napkins, a table, etc.).

What's your favorite smoothie? What would you choose if you had to choose between a strawberry banana smoothie and a chocolate banana smoothie? Do you like smoothies or shakes more?

  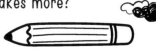

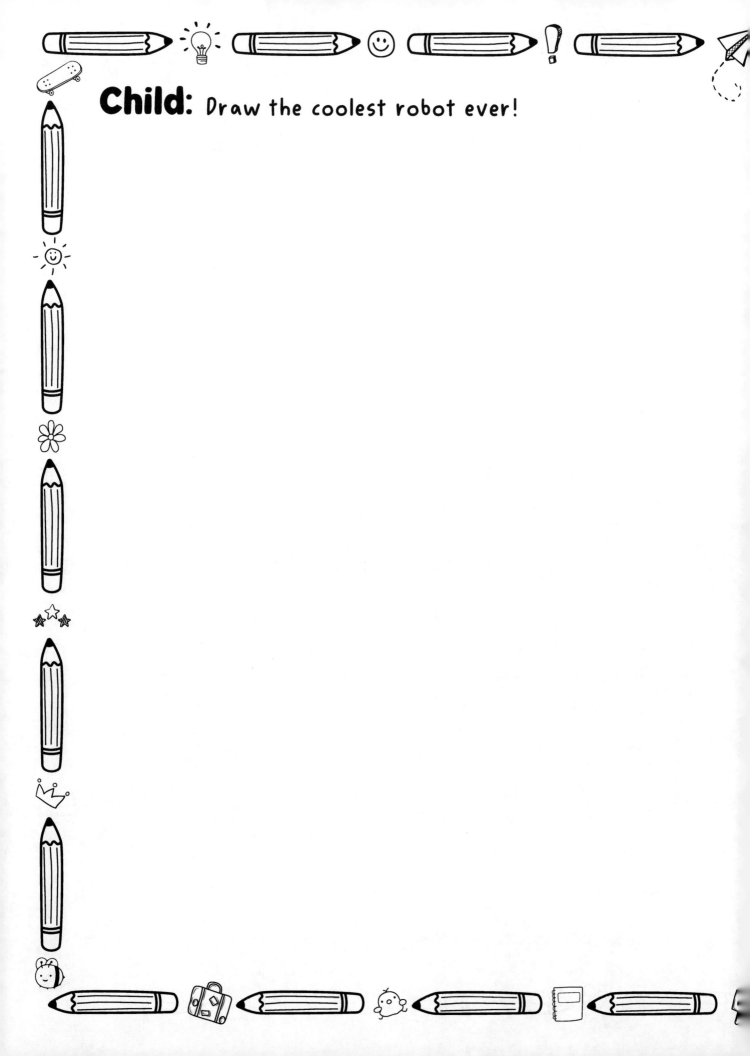

Child: Draw the coolest robot ever!

Mom: Draw a few features for the robot. Then draw what the robot can do (mustache, unibrow... cooks, rides a skateboard, etc.).

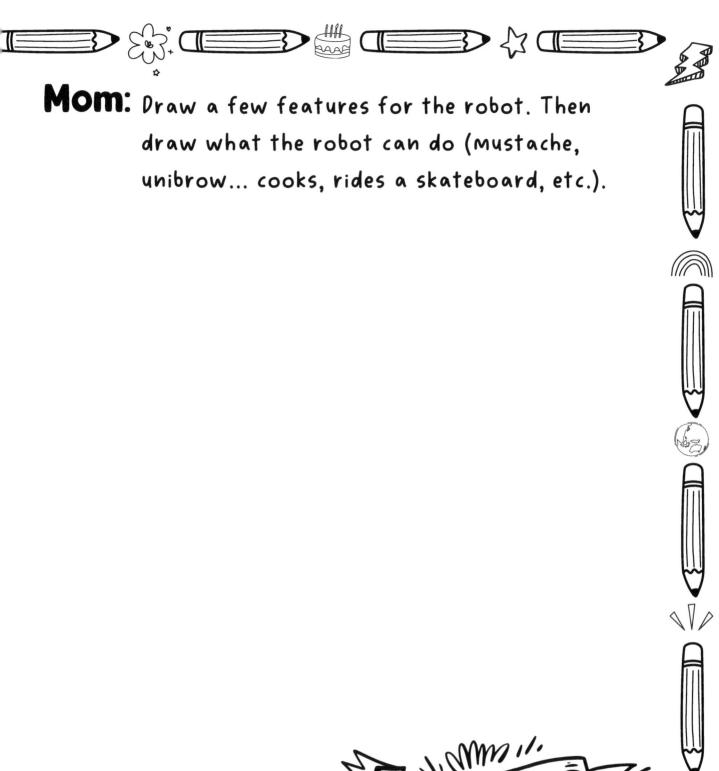

(ROBOT'S NAME)

What would you want your robot to do? Do you think there will be flying robots in the future?

Child: If dragons existed what would they look like? Draw the dragon's head, body, and legs.

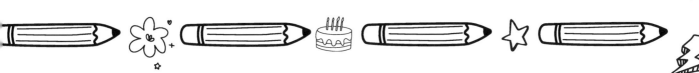

Mom: Draw the dragon's wings (if they have any) and tail.

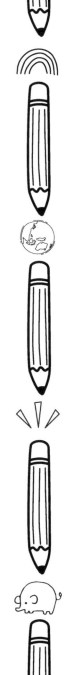

°Do you think dragons can fly? Do you think they have powers and are they friendly? If you had a pet dragon, and named it after the last thing you ate, what would it's name be?

Child: Let's turn the book and draw the biggest cake ever!

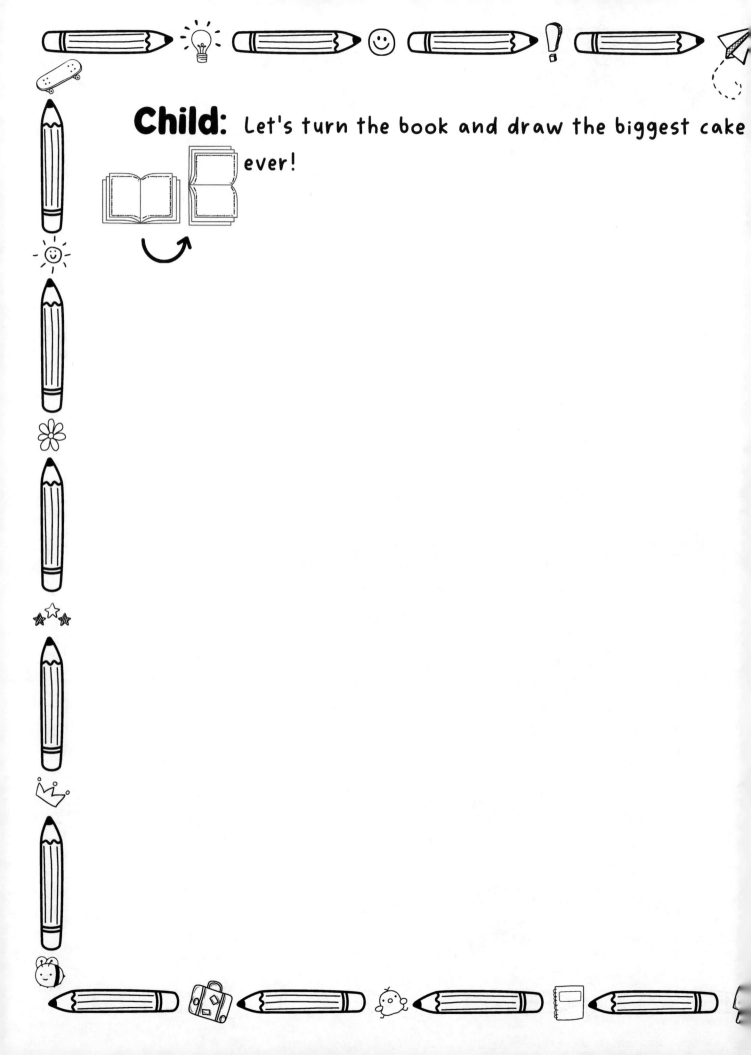

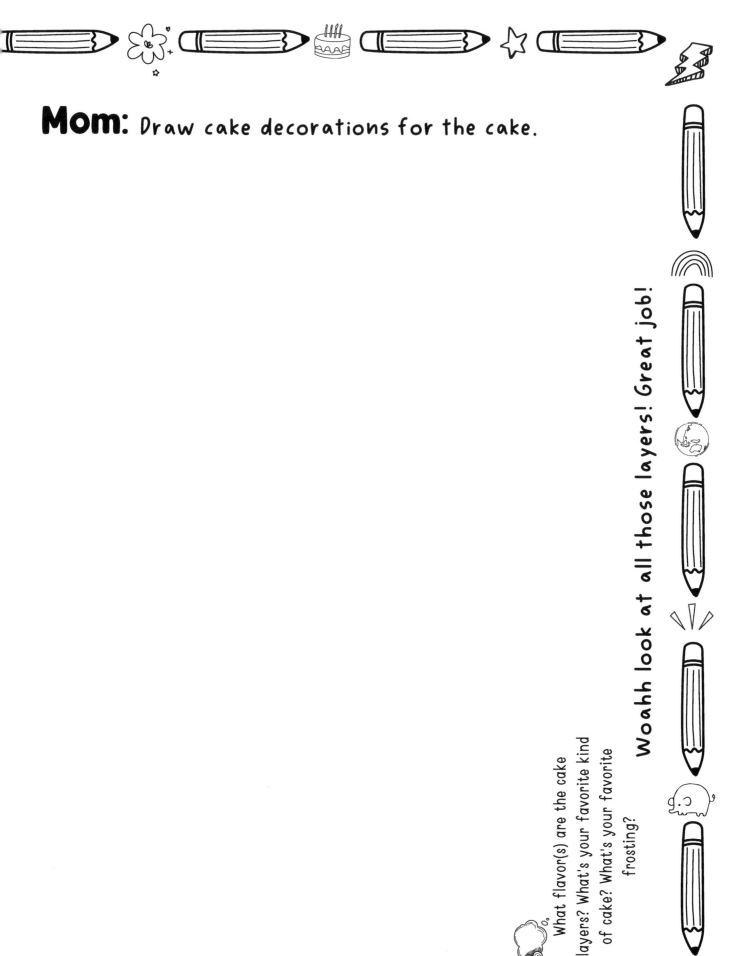

Mom: Draw cake decorations for the cake.

What flavor(s) are the cake layers? What's your favorite kind of cake? What's your favorite frosting?

Woahh look at all those layers! Great job!

Child: Let's pretend to take a trip to outer space! Draw you and your mom as astronauts.

Mom: Draw some things you might find in outer space (planets, stars, the moon, aliens, etc.).

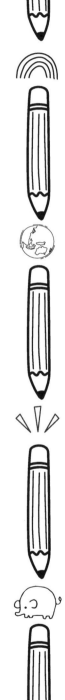

Do you think aliens are real? If so, what would they look like? Do you think the moon is made out of cheese?

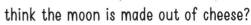

Child: An astronaut needs a spaceship! Draw a spaceship.

Mom: Come up with a destination for your spaceship. Draw that destination.

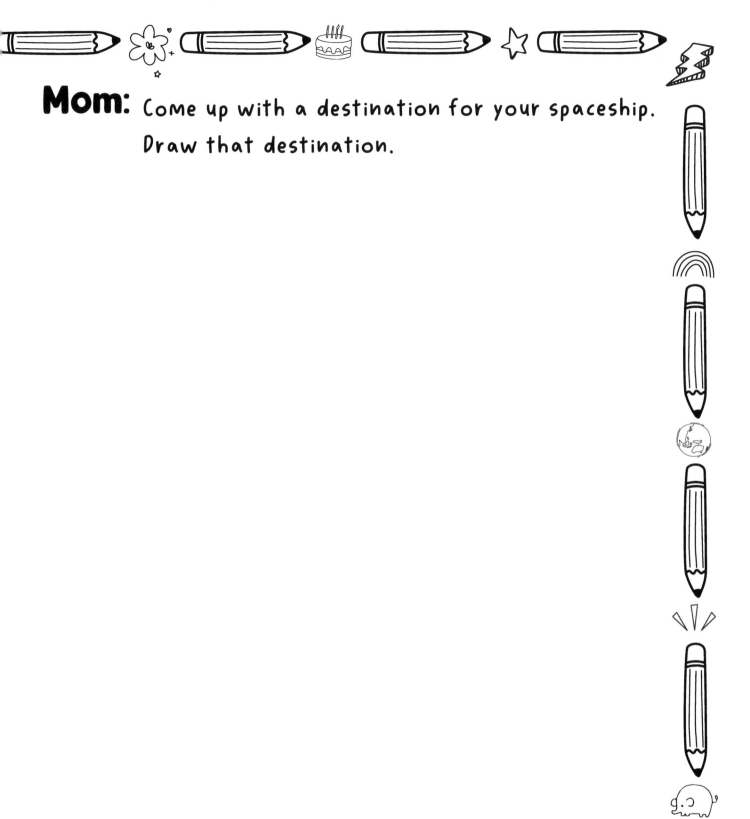

If you could visit any planet, which planet would it be and why? What's your favorite planet?

Child: Let's pretend to spend the day at the beach with Mom! Draw a few things you would bring to the beach and a few things you might find at the beach.

Mom: Draw a few beach activities (like surfing, volleyball, campfire, fishing, sand castles, etc.).

How many beaches have you been to? What's your favorite beach? What are some fun beach memories you have?

Child: Look it's a bird, it's a plane, it's a new superhero?! Invent and draw this amazing new superhero.

Mom: Draw the superhero's superpowers. Draw someone in need of help.

Superhero name:

Superpowers:

Identification Card

If you could have a superpower, what would it be? Who's your favorite superhero?

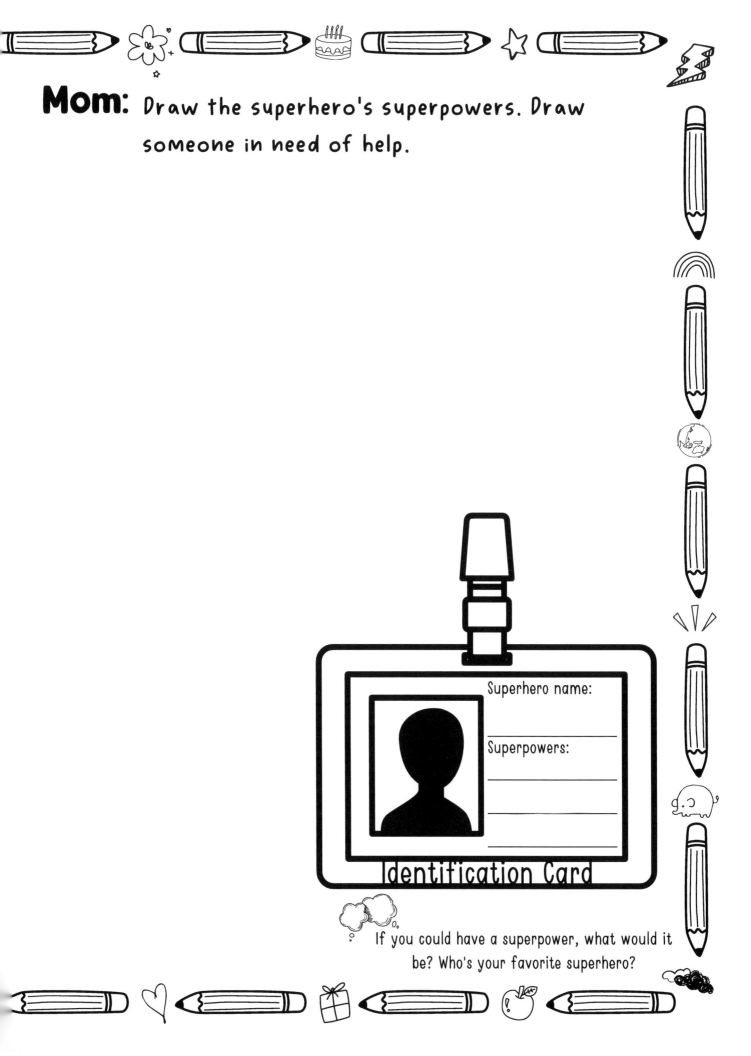

Child: Time for ice cream! Let's turn the book and draw the biggest ice cream scoops ever.

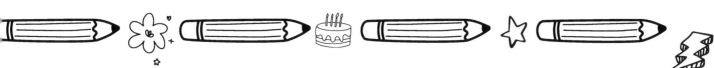

Mom: Draw the ice cream cone and use both of your favorite candies as toppings.

Wow! Look at those humongous scoops!

What is your favorite ice cream flavor? Do you like eating ice cream in a bowl or a cone? What are your favorite ice cream toppings?

Child: Draw your favorite vehicle.

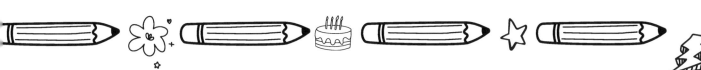

Mom: Draw your favorite vehicle next to theirs.

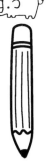

Would you rather ride a bike or ride a scooter? Do you like trains or planes more? Do you like boats or cars more?

  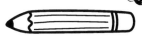

Child: Let's pretend to make a potion! Draw a few items that will go into the potion.

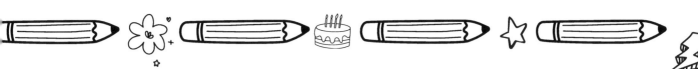

Mom: Add a few more items for the potion (like spinach, eye of newt, a stinky sock, etc.). Draw a vile for your potion and a cauldron.

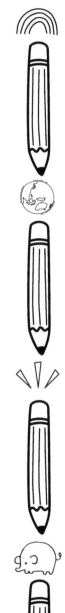

 How do you take the potion? Do you drink it, smell it, rub it on your hands? What happens to the person that takes this potion?!

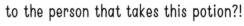

   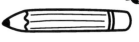

Child: If you could have any pet you wanted, what would it be? Draw that pet down below!

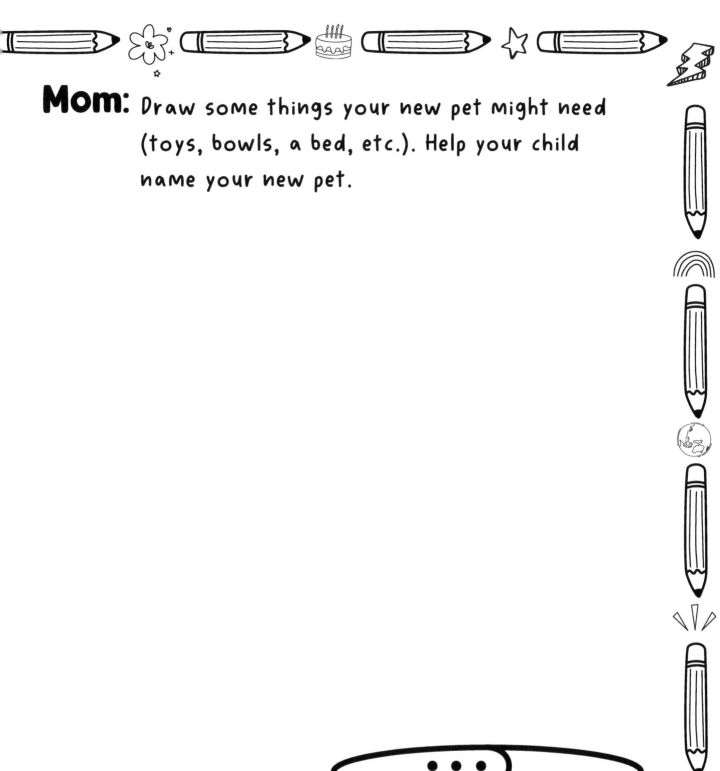

Mom: Draw some things your new pet might need (toys, bowls, a bed, etc.). Help your child name your new pet.

(new pet's name)

Do you have any pets? Mom, did you have any pets when you were little? If so, can you share a memory of that pet? What is the best thing about having a pet?

Child: Ahoy there! Let's pretend to go on an adventure to find the missing treasure with Mom! First, we have to have a map! Draw a big map. Draw a circle to show the starting point. Then start drawing some obstacles and landmarks around your map.

Mom: x marks the spot! Mark the x where the treasure is. Add more landmarks if needed. Then draw the trail line from the starting point, through the obstacles and landmarks, to the x.

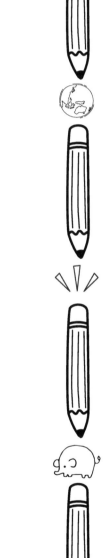

What would you pack for the adventure?
What do you think the treasure is?

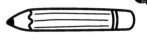

Child: Great job, that map looks AMAZINGGG! Now how will you get to the treasure? Draw what you will use to get to the treasure.

Need help?

Here are some ideas: a boat, plane, car, helicopter, giant bird, or a flying burrito.

Mom: Draw the scenery. Draw some special features to add to your special mode of transportation (for example, if your child comes up with a flying donut, maybe it has a sprinkle blaster).

Do you think you will encounter any mysterious creatures along the way? Have you ever gone on a treasure or scavenger hunt?

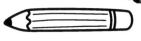

Child: Oh no! Along the way, you get attacked by the silliest monsters ever. But it's okay because you have a secret weapon! Draw your secret weapon.

Need help?

Here are some ideas: maybe you have donuts that these monsters can't resist and by eating them, they fall asleep! Or maybe it's a pair of stinky socks that can be used to scare them away! Anythin can be a secret weapon!

Mom: Draw those silly monsters.

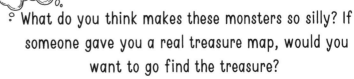

What do you think makes these monsters so silly? If someone gave you a real treasure map, would you want to go find the treasure?

Child: You guys did it! You found the treasure!!! What do you and your mom want the treasure to be? Draw your treasure.

Mom: Draw the treasure box and add more detail to their drawing (trees, sand, animals, etc.).

If you found a real treasure chest, what would you want to find inside?

Child: When it gets windy outside, do you think flying a kite would be a great activity? Draw a big kite flying high in the sky.

Mom: Draw a long string and some bows for your kite. Draw you and your child flying the kite. Add more detail to the background (a hill, clouds, the sun, etc.).

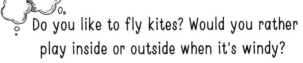
Do you like to fly kites? Would you rather play inside or outside when it's windy?

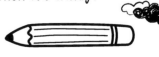

Child: Let's draw a magnificent castle!

Mom: Every castle needs a queen and their prince or princess, draw you and your little royal highness. Then draw the landscape for the castle.

What's your favorite fairytale? What do you like about it? If you got to live in a castle where would you want the castle to be: in the forest, in the mountains, in outer space, or overlooking the sea?

Child: Let's pretend to have a movie night! Can you draw a scene from your favorite movie?

Mom: Draw a few things you like to have when you watch movies (snacks, blankets, pillows, etc.).

What's your favorite movie? Do you like kettle corn or butter popcorn more? What is your all-time favorite movie snack? Is there a movie you want to try watching together sometime?

Child: Would you rather be cold or hot? Do you like seeing leaves falling or flowers blooming more? Draw your favorite season.

Mom: Draw your favorite season.

What do you like about your favorite season? If you
could invent a new season what would it be like?

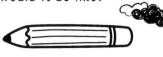

Child: Let's pretend you're going on a road trip with Mom! Draw a few things you would want to pack for your road trip.

Mom: Draw a few more things you would pack for the road trip.

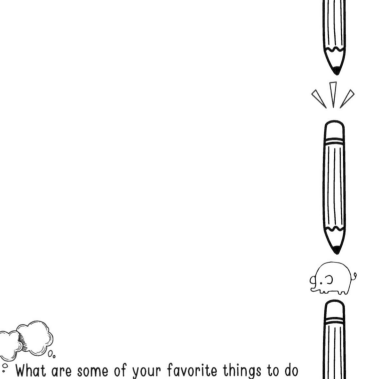

What are some of your favorite things to do when you are on a road trip? What are your favorite road trip games? What are some of your favorite road trip snacks?

Child: Let's turn the book and draw a ginormous tree house! Draw the giant tree.

Mom: Draw the tree house (tire swing, rope, ladder, pulley system for snacks, etc.).

That is one GIANT tree!

If you had your own treehouse, what would you put inside? What kinds of activities would you like to do in your tree house?

Child: Do you like to go on vacations? Draw a few things you would pack for a vacation.

Mom: Draw a few more items to pack, then draw a few different vehicles you and your child could take to travel.

What are some of your favorite vacation memories? Where would you like to go on your next vacation? What vehicle would you like to take to get there?

Child: Let's pretend to camp out in the living room! Draw a giant fort.

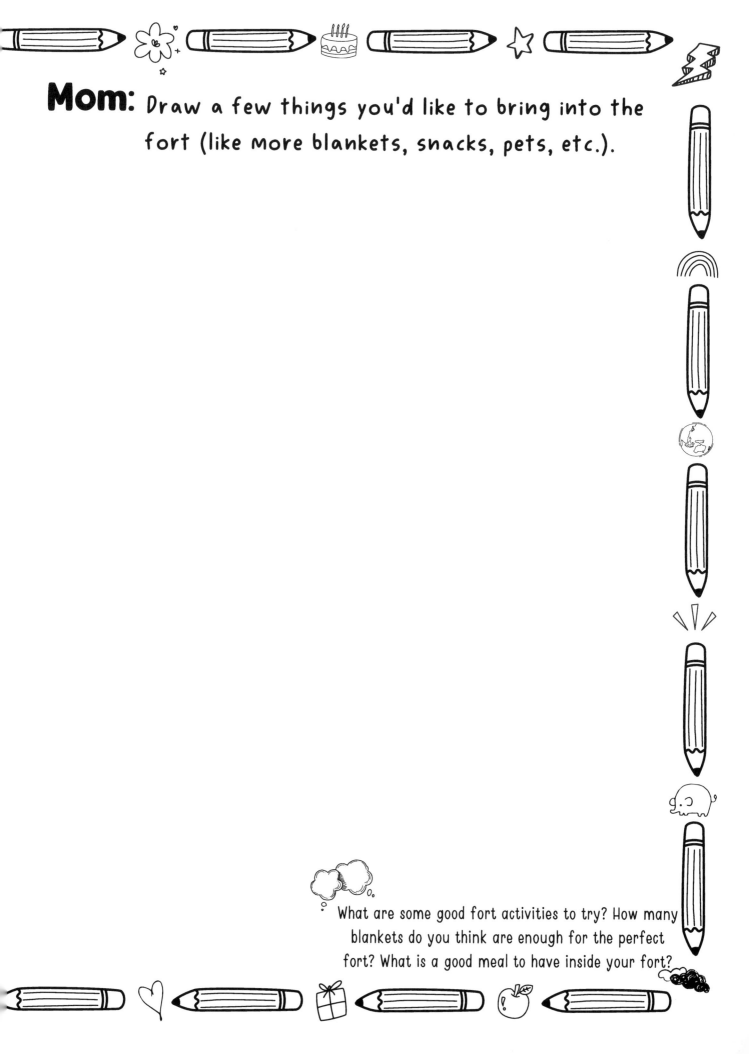

Mom: Draw a few things you'd like to bring into the fort (like more blankets, snacks, pets, etc.).

What are some good fort activities to try? How many blankets do you think are enough for the perfect fort? What is a good meal to have inside your fort?

Child: Have you ever been on an airplane? If so where did you get to go? Let's draw an airplane!

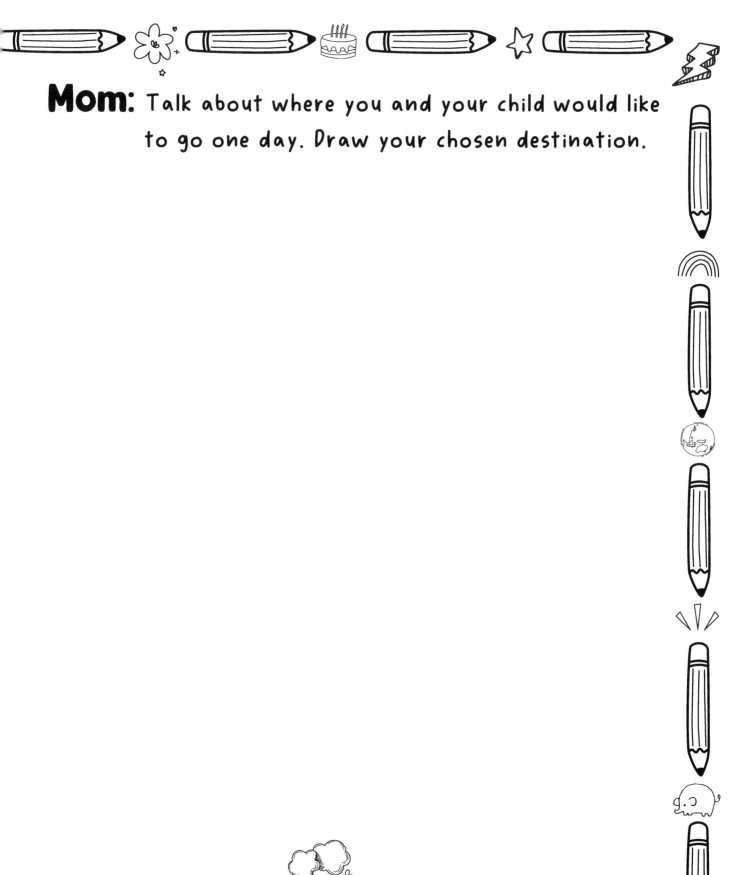

Mom: Talk about where you and your child would like to go one day. Draw your chosen destination.

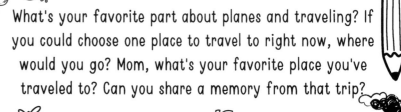

What's your favorite part about planes and traveling? If you could choose one place to travel to right now, where would you go? Mom, what's your favorite place you've traveled to? Can you share a memory from that trip?

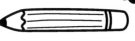

Child: Home is a great place to be! Your toys are there, your room is awesome, and most importantly your family is there. Draw your family.

Mom: Draw your family's home.

What do you like most about each other? Name one thing you are proud of yourself for, and then write below one thing that makes you proud of the other person.

I am proud of mom because: _____

_____

I am proud of _____ because: _____
(child)

_____

Child: Let's pretend to be spies! Create a special symbol, so that whenever Mom sees it, she's the only person that knows it's you. Draw it below.

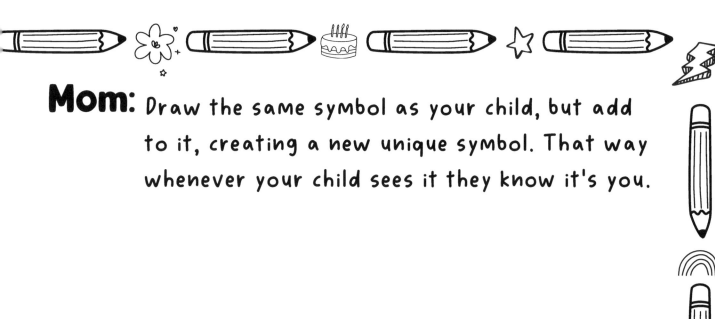

Mom: Draw the same symbol as your child, but add to it, creating a new unique symbol. That way whenever your child sees it they know it's you.

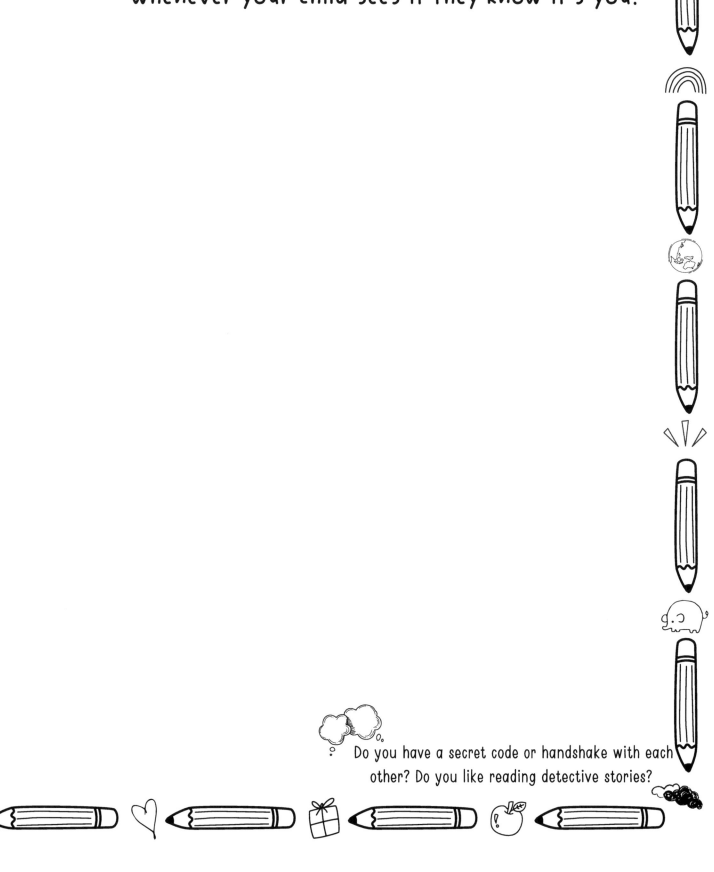

Do you have a secret code or handshake with each other? Do you like reading detective stories?

Child: Let's pretend to have a race! Draw two race cars racing.

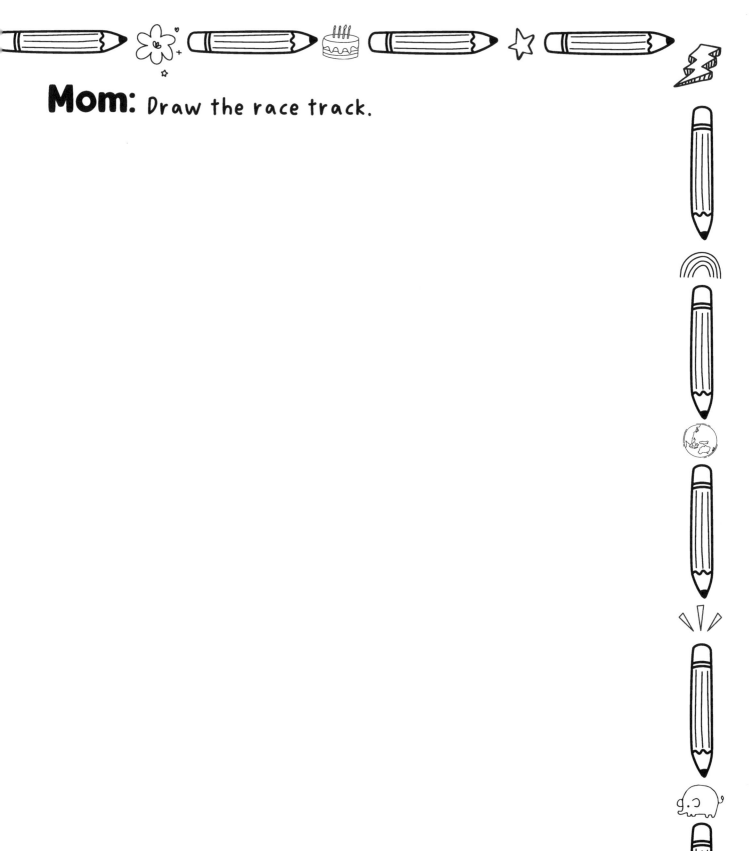

Mom: Draw the race track.

Do you like to have contests and competitions? What's your favorite type of contest or competition?

Child: Let's pretend you and your mom are on a trip to the zoo! Draw a few animals that can be found at the zoo.

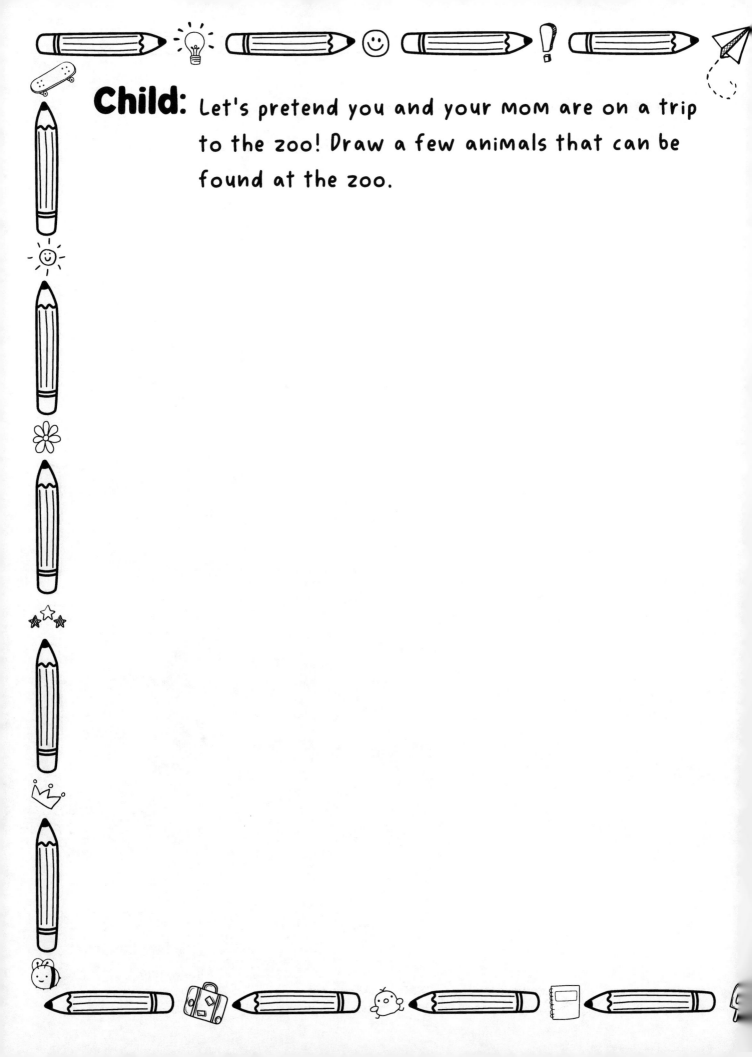

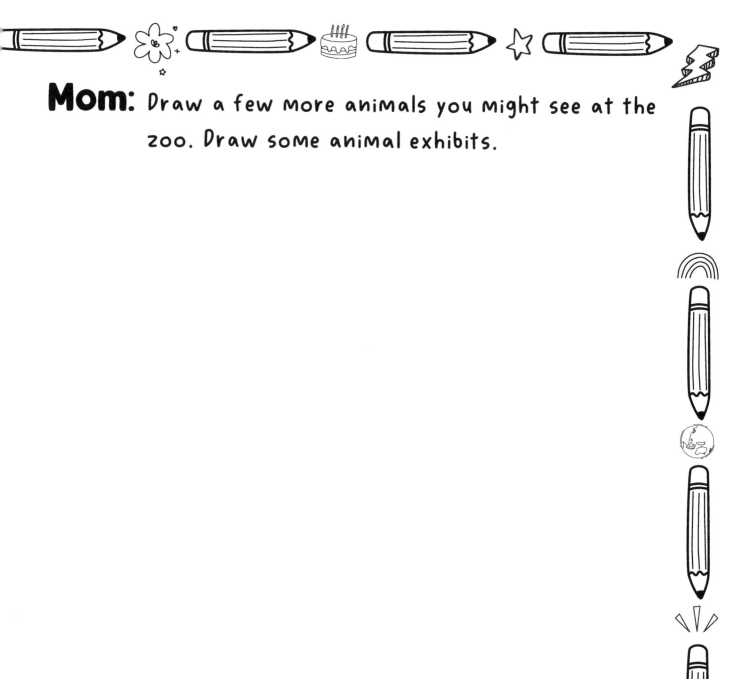

Mom: Draw a few more animals you might see at the zoo. Draw some animal exhibits.

Do you like going to the zoo more or the aquarium? What's the first animal exhibit you like to see when you get to the zoo?

Child: Wow, what is that? While you're at the zoo, there looks to be a new species of animal! Can you invent and draw that new animal?

Need help? → Think about how many legs it might have. Does it have hair? Is it a land, sea, or flying animal? What does it eat? What color is it

Mom: Draw your child's new animal habitat.

What is your favorite animal to see at the zoo? What do you like about them?

Child: What do you do with seeds? That's right you plant them! Let's draw a beautiful garden! Draw a few things you would want to grow.

Mom: Draw a few more plants to grow. Draw you and your child planting together.

If you could grow a plant in real life, what plant would that be? Would you rather grow veggies or fruit?

Child: Draw your favorite meal and see if Mom can guess what it is. Was she right?!

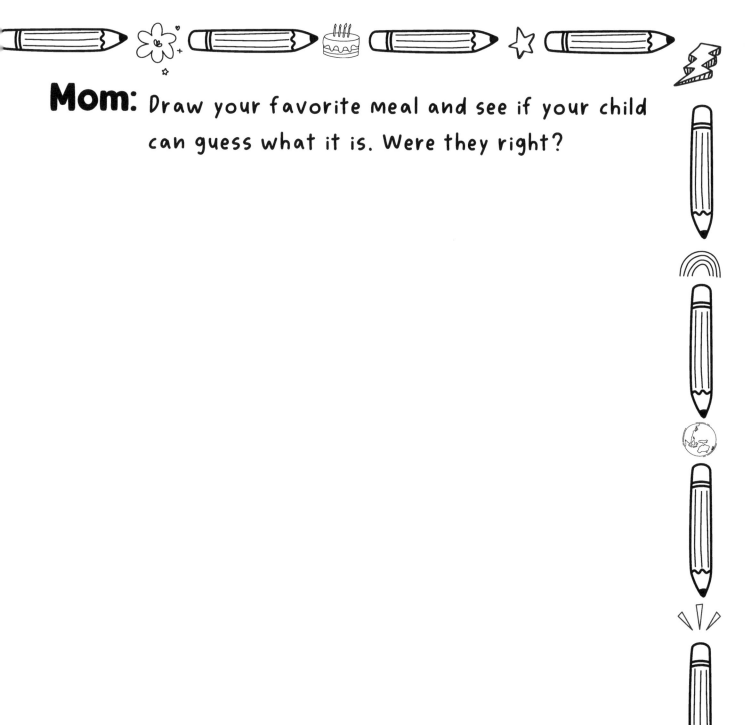

Mom: Draw your favorite meal and see if your child can guess what it is. Were they right?

If you had to eat the same thing every day, what would you eat? What is your least favorite food? When is your favorite mealtime?

Child: If you had to choose an animal that represents (reminds you of) your mom, what animal would that be? Draw that animal below.

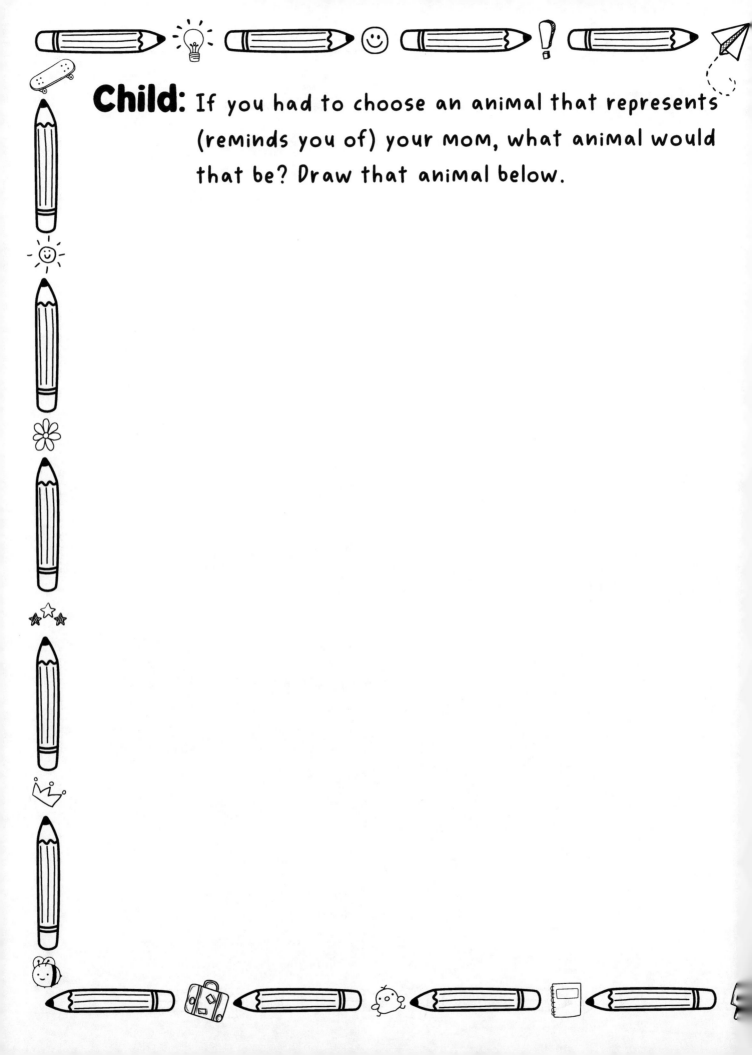

Mom: If you had to choose an animal that represents your child, what animal would that be? Draw that animal below.

Why did you choose the animal you chose for each other? What kind of unique qualities does that animal have that you also see in the other person? (ex. tiger... because mom is brave like a tiger!)

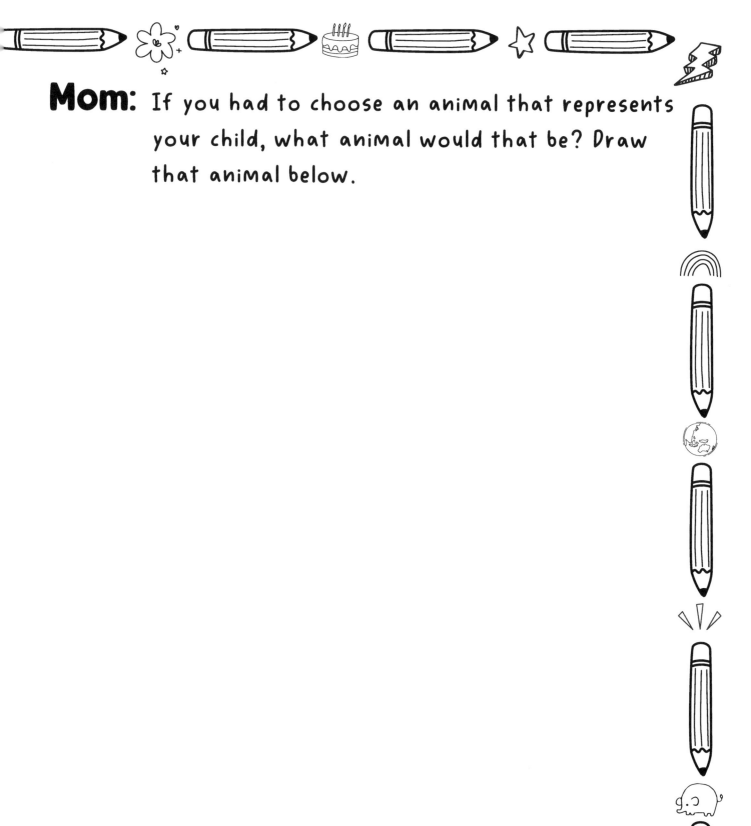

Child: Let's draw a giant pizza. Then draw a line down the middle of the pizza. Pick one side of your pizza and draw a few of your favorite toppings.

Mom: Fill the other half of the pizza with your favorite toppings. Draw plates, napkins, and cups.

What type of pizza crust is your favorite?
Where is your favorite place to get pizza?
Does pineapple belong on pizza?

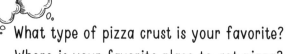

Child: Let's pretend to go on a picnic with Mom! Draw a few things you would pack for a picnic.

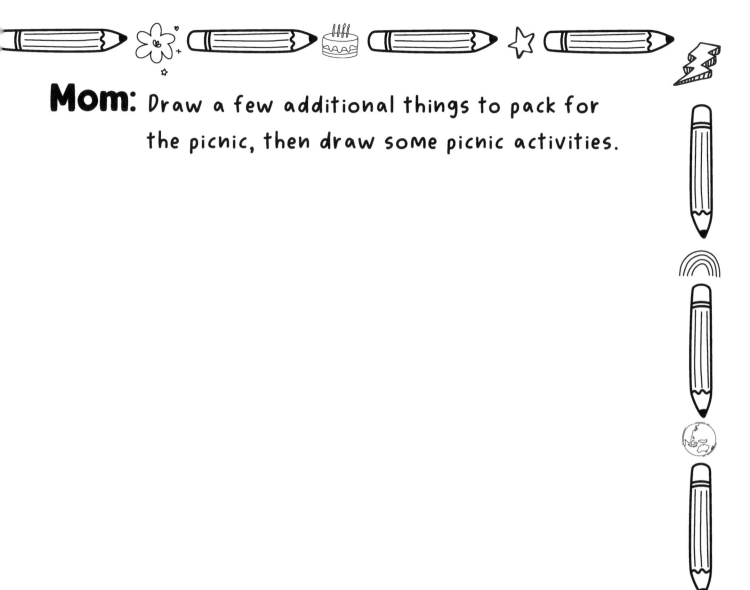

Mom: Draw a few additional things to pack for the picnic, then draw some picnic activities.

Would you rather have a picnic at the park or a picnic in the forest? Would you rather have pizza or sandwiches to eat during your picnic?

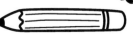

Child: Let's pretend to take a dive into the sea! Draw a few animals you might see in the ocean.

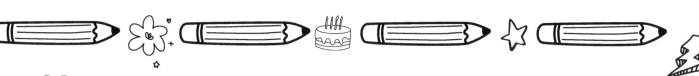

Mom: Draw a few items you might see in the sea (shipwreck, treasure chest, pearls, coral reef, etc.). Draw you and your child scuba diving.

What's your favorite sea animal, and why? How long do you think you can hold your breath underwater? If you could swim with sharks, would you do it?

Child: Let's pretend to go on a safari adventure! Before we go, we need to pack a few things. Draw a few things you and your mom will need for the trip.

Mom: Draw a few additional items you would want to pack, then draw the land rover you will be taking.

 Which animal would you want to see first on your safari adventure? Is there an animal you would not want to see?

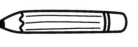

Child: Wow, you packed some great stuff, good job! Woah, look at all those animals! Draw a few animals you might see on safari.

Mom: Draw the landscape of your safari trip (a waterhole, a few trees, a swamp, etc.).

 Would you rather see elephants or giraffes? Lions or cheetahs? Snakes or crocodiles?

Child: That was so much fun! Let's pretend to travel to a new place, how about the jungle?! Draw a few animals and plants you might see in the jungle.

Mom: Draw more plants and animals found in the jungle. Then draw you and your child exploring.

Can you name a movie that takes place in the jungle? If you could be an animal that lives in the jungle, what would it be and why?

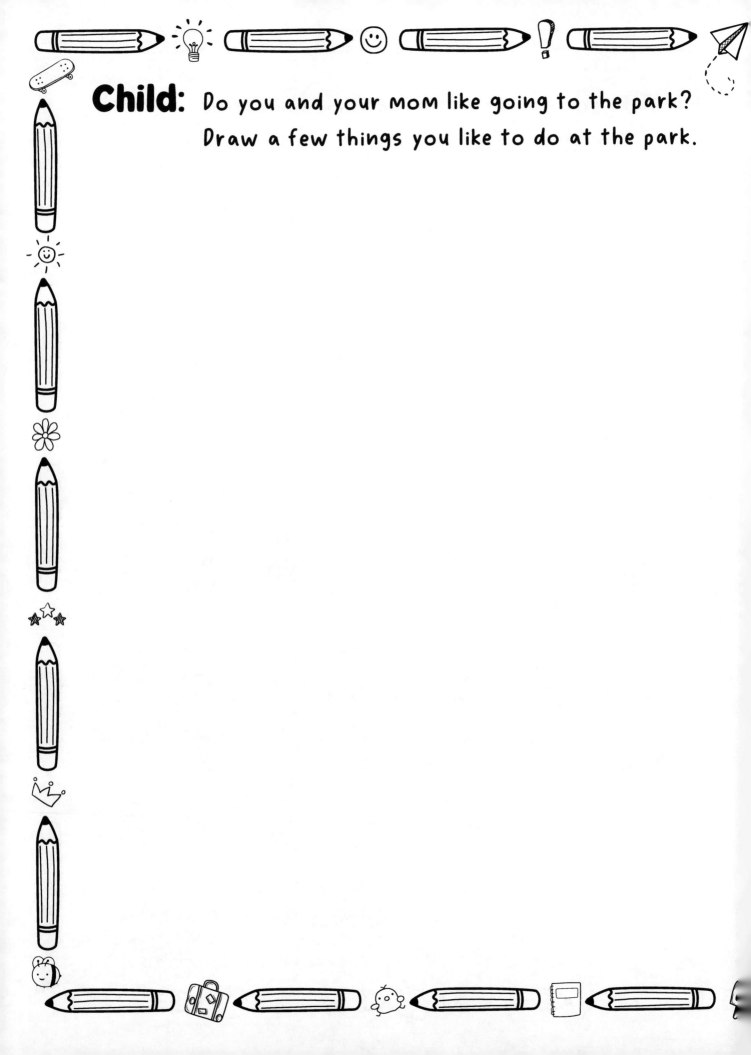

Child: Do you and your mom like going to the park? Draw a few things you like to do at the park.

Mom: Draw the park's landscape (playground, picnic tables, fields, etc.).

What's your favorite thing to do at the park? Would you rather roll down a big hill or play on the playground?

Child: Let's pretend to go on a frosty adventure. Can you guess where? You're going to the Arctic! Draw a few things you will need for the Arctic.

Mom: Draw a few additional items needed for the trip, then draw the plane or boat that you will use to get to the Arctic.

 How cold do you think it is in the Arctic? If you could really go there, would you want to?

Child: Wow, you packed well! Now you and Mom will be nice and warm! Look at those beautiful animals! Can you draw a few animals you might see in the Arctic?

Mom: Draw a few icebergs, an igloo, and the ocean.

Which animal that lives in the Arctic is your favorite? Would you rather be cold or hot?

Child: Do you like to learn about sea life? What place can you go to see sea creatures? That's right smarty, the aquarium! Draw a few animals you might see at the aquarium.

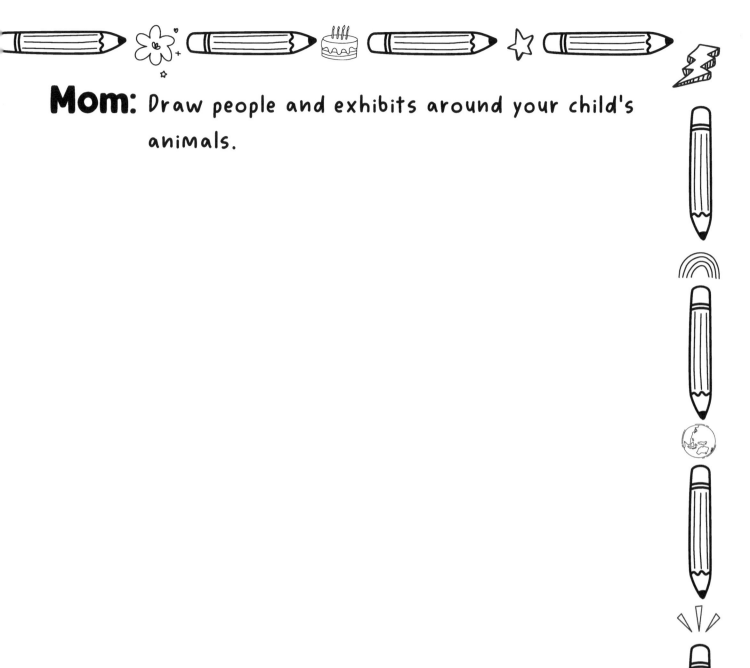

Mom: Draw people and exhibits around your child's animals.

What is your favorite exhibit at the aquarium? What animal do you look forward to seeing the most at the aquarium? If you could touch a sea animal, which one would you choose?

Child: Did you hear that? Rumble... RUMble... RUMBLE! ROARRRRR! Eek! It's a dinosaur! Draw the head and the body of the biggest dinosaur ever!

Mom: Draw the dinosaur's limbs and tail.

Do you have a favorite dinosaur? If so what it is and why? If you could, would you want to meet a real-life dinosaur? Can you roar like a dinosaur? If so let's hear it!

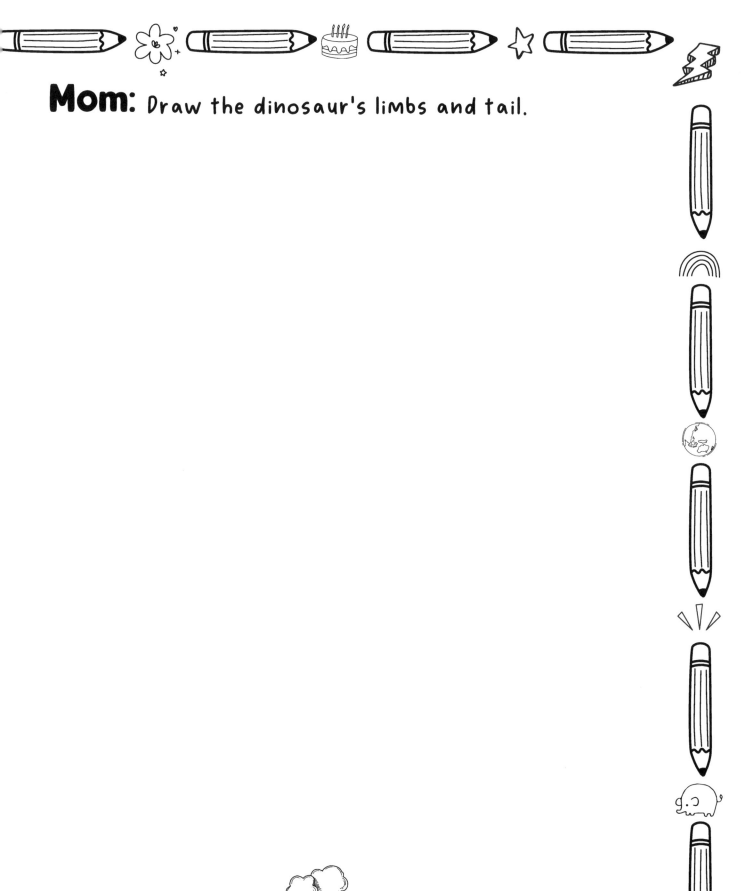

Child: Draw your favorite sport.

Mom: Draw your favorite sport as a child.

What do/did you like about your favorite sport? Do you or anyone else in your family play sports? Mom, have you ever played a team sport? Did you win any trophies?

Child: Let's pretend to go on a camping trip with Mom! Let's pack up the car! Draw a few items you'd like to take on the camping trip.

Mom: Draw a few additional essential camping items, then draw your car.

Have you ever gone camping before? If so where? What are a few of your favorite camping memories? Would you rather camp in the forest or by a lake?

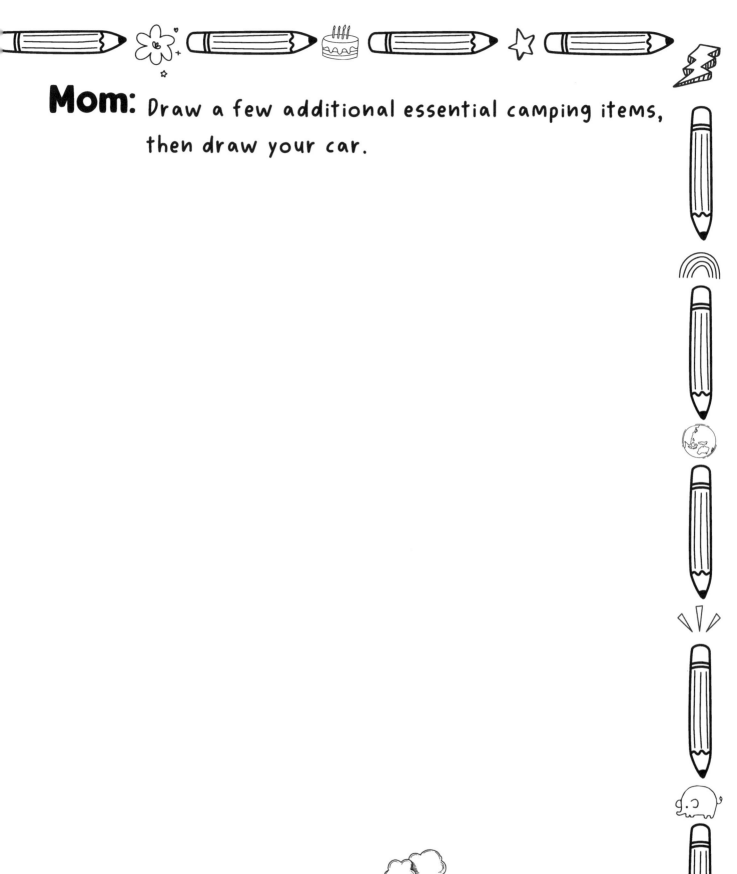

Child: Great job packing kiddo! Let's choose a campsite and set up. Would you want to camp in the forest, beach, or backyard? Draw a tent and a campfire.

Mom: Draw where you and your child decided to go camping.

Do you like being outdoors? What are some of your favorite outdoor activities?

Child: What a fun adventure! Draw a few camping activities.

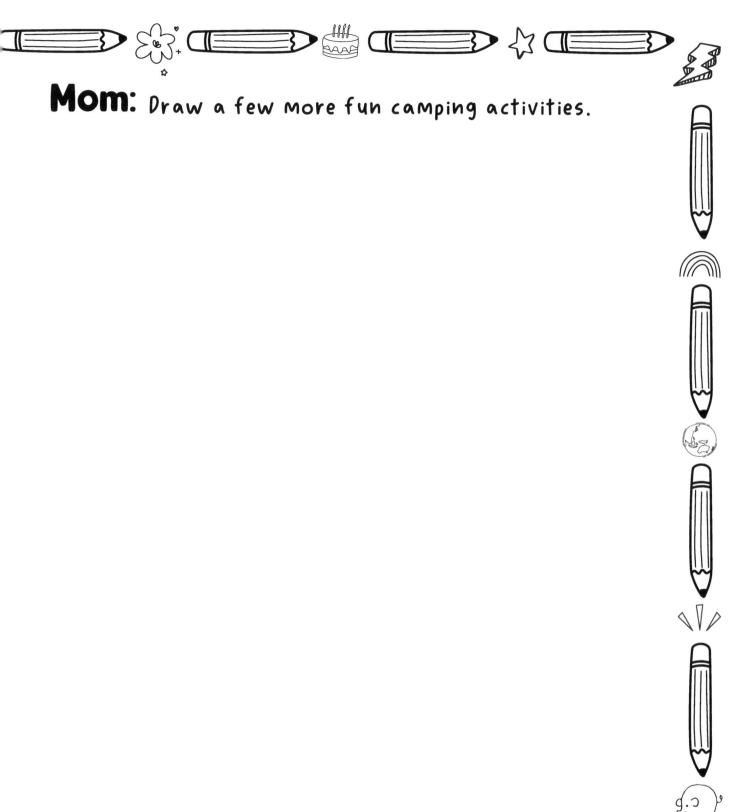

Mom: Draw a few more fun camping activities.

Do you like camping? Would you rather sleep in a tent or in a cabin?

    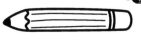

Take turns drawing the other person inside of the frame, to celebrate completing this book's very last drawing!

and

_____   _____
(name)   (name)

We made some amazing memories together and finished this book on _____
(date)

A few things to look back on one day...

What was one of your favorite memories you had, while you and your mom were drawing in this book?

_____

_____

Mom, what was one of your favorite memories?

_____

_____

Write down something new you learned about each other while using this book.

_____
(Child)

_____
(Mom)

What was your favorite picture you drew together?

_____
(Child)

_____
(Mom)

Certificate of Recognition

presented to

_____
(child)

on the _____ of _____
(day)   (mm/yyyy)

For trying their best in completing this book!

Signed by: _____
(mom)

Certificate of Recognition

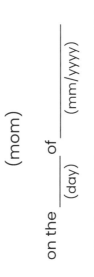

presented to

_____
(mom)

on the _____ of _____
(day)   (mm/yyyy)

For trying their best in completing this book!

Signed by: _____
(child)

thank you!

Did you enjoy this book? If you have a moment, please consider giving us a review! Not only does it tremendously help us grow, it also helps us make more of what you like!

★ ★ ★ ★ ★

WE WOULD LOVE TO SEE YOUR ARTWORK! On your review please consider sending in a picture of one of your favorite creations!

Thanks for your support! ♡